Ode to Gaia
Calling Forth our Imaginal Selves

Ode to Gaia: Calling Forth our Imaginal Selves
By Deborah J Milton, PhD

www.deborahmiltonartist.com
www.awakeningstorylines.com

Copyright @ 2018 by Deborah J Milton
All Rights Reserved
Please treat this material with respect.
No part of this publication may be reproduced,
stored in a retrieval system or transmitted in any form
or by any means or conveyed via the internet
without prior written permission,
except in the case of brief references
which identify the artist/author
and include contact information.
Please contact the author/artist
if you want permission for extensive use.
Thank you.

ISBN -13:
978-1986707244

ISBN-10:
1986707245

To the magnificence...

*Life calls for reverence,
celebrating
our existence
on this planetary home
in our galactic neighborhood*

*Let it be acknowledged
that we are
all natives
to this earth*

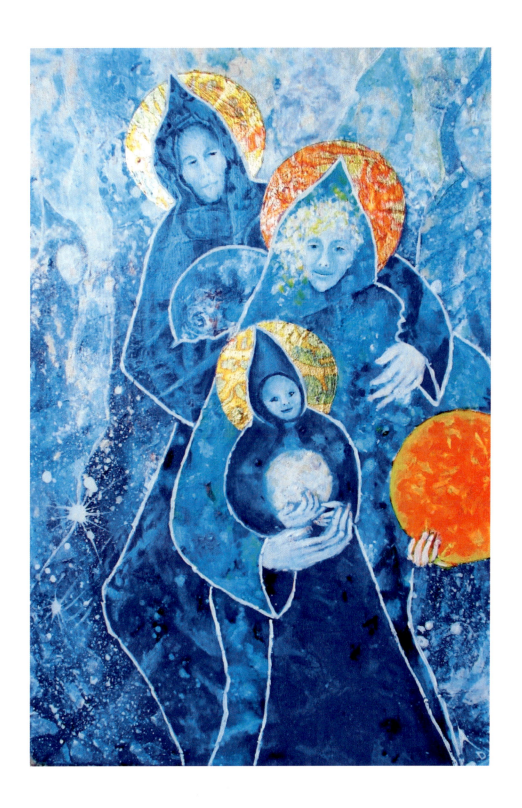

*This ancient living system eARTh
is a babe born
from the infinite cosmic womb,
revered by our human ancestors
who wait for our return*

*Though we meddle, pillage and deny,
in our gut we know
we are beholden*

*Our lives completely and
utterly dependent
on what Gaia,
our motherfathergodde
provides*

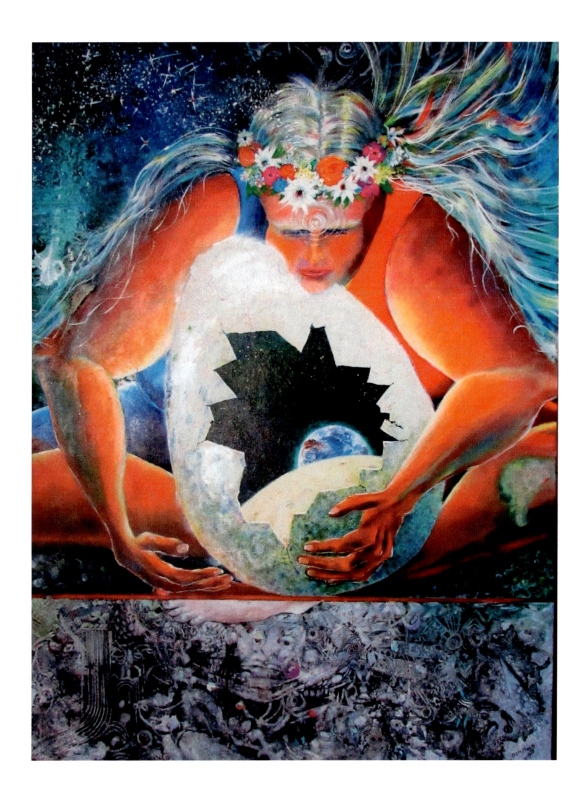

One Source
known by many names:
Gaia,
Great Mystery,
Li & Qi,
God,
Creator,
Infinite Universe,
Tao

Gaia
inexplicable
life force energy

Embedded in the whole shebang we are!

*Galaxies
literally spin
in my body,
your body,
their bodies,
all bodies*

*We modern humans have lost
our sense of the miraculous*

*Our early ancestors
knew everywhere & everything
as
dancing, pulsing, shimmering, living
Gaia*

*We responded to the flight of birds,
witnessed the bear
searching for medicine plants,
noticed the migration of caribou and wildebeest.*

*We heard messages on the wind,
watched the moon's repetitive changes,
made note of the unerring path of the sun,
lived according to the seasons.*

*We knew that we belonged
to the community of life
on this planet.*

But now...

...I mourn our loneliness
as I sit on a whacked off
silvered stump
in the clear cut
old growth temperate rainforest,
this devastated spot
once a rainbow of greens
with trickling, seeping, gurgling,
bubbling
waters spawning life.

It only takes a year
for these wrecked miles
to turn grey upon grey,
life bleached out of the landscape
by sun's unfiltered fire.

I ask these stumps
rooted to their dying soil,
"How are we 21st century humans
like you?"

"Severed from your roots you are,"
my more-than-human ancestor
immediately responds.
"Remember your magnificence.
You are born from this Gaian miracle."

*I weep sudden tears for the logger,
whose soul must stagger in anguish
as she makes the first cut
to demolish the source
of her own breathing*

*We hasten our own demise
by closing our eyes
to the truth of our dependency*

*Forgive us
for knowing NOT what we do!*

*But wait...
We can choose to remember!*

*Like the butterfly's imaginal cells
transforming the caterpillar,
we can be humanity's imaginal selves,
re-storying possibilities
to ensure our future.*

*What if we chose love
as our true compass?
With love as our guide,
everything changes*

What if we chose wonder?

*Such a blessing to tremble in awe,
to know in our bones
that our lives here/now
are the most recent chapter
in a story 13.7 billion years old*

What if we chose to acknowledge
that everything else
enriches our human lives
in countless ways?

Do I really need to make a list?

Really?

Think about it.
We are nothing without everything else,
everyone else.

No thing at all

*What if we chose the wisdom of ecstasy,
experiencing the fullness of
no longer being encapsulated by our skins?*

This expanded awareness changes everything

*What if we chose to create
new patterns of meaning…
new stories, songs and spiritual inspiration
rooted in Gaia's natural systems…*

*What if we chose to restory
religion, economics, science, and ethics,
chose to redefine
power, success, and happiness?*

What if we chose to put limits on ourselves?

*Imagine we humans
choosing
NOT to act
like a cancer
consuming its host,
but instead
choosing
to be
an imaginal cell,
an imaginal self,
devoted to transforming
a ravenous, rampaging
caterpillar culture
to a
compassionate, creative, celebratory
butterfly culture?*

What if we dedicated
our intelligence and imagination
to nourishing all life...
all our ecosystems,
which,
if you think about it,
helps
everyone
and
everything
thrive.

I said something similar
on page 44,
but it bears repeating

What if we all remembered
that
sharing makes life easier for everyone,
honesty *is* the best policy,
and
the biggest bully is really a terrified kid?

Everything would change.

Our planetary home,
a radiant jewel
spinning in the vastness,
has many more years of experience
nourishing life
than we do.

It's time to listen
to our Mother, Gaia.

As you color in this image, imagine how you could nurture your own imaginal self.

How do you envision the ECO-centric human? Write or draw here if you wish. What colors, patterns, textures, shapes, lines, images, words carry the essence for YOU? Feel free to risk! Explore! Dive in...Play for at least 10 minutes.

Thank you for spending time with my vision.
I hope it inspires your own. The world needs more and more of us imaginal selves
to show up and be counted, to share our wisdom, to realign ourselves
with the sacred nature of all life and to midwife the birth of a new version of our species.
Together we can do this!
The following few pages are my testimony to the power of community,
whether it be virtual or face to face. Please join in wherever you are called.

You can learn more about me, Deborah J Milton, at these two sites:
http://deborahmiltonartist.com
http://awakeningstorylines.com
To learn more about caterpillar soup and imaginal cells,
https://awakeningstorylines.com/2018/05/28/imaginal-selves/

Here, too, are several YouTubes I've made:
From Grief to Grace - the power of intuitive painting to heal
https://www.youtube.com/watch?v=xUJ7e-mVF6U

Making ARTful Prayers:
http://youtu.be/6TiTs-0c3Ww

Webinar - The Wisdom of Ecstasy:
https://www.youtube.com/watch?v=FDi3HCiTxIE

My friend **Jean Anthony** sings and makes videos which feature women's artwork,
including mine: Check out **Goddess Woman Tree** http://vimeo.com/92885695

I am full of gratitude for living in the age of the www:
I want to acknowledge people I would never have met without the world wide web.
I stand on their shoulders, as perhaps you will stand on mine.
Two Australians have inspired me with online classes, and feel like global kin.
Jassy Watson, eARThist, taught me the process of **Painting Gaia** and changed
the course of my artistic life. Formally trained as an artist, she is also a grounded woman
and inspired/inspiring teacher. You can meet her here:
http://www.earthcirclestudios.com/

Glenys Livingstone, PhD, author and ceremonialist, co-facilitated with Jassy.
Glenys has written several books. I highly recommend:
PaGaian Cosmology – Re-inventing Earth-based Goddess Religion.
Meet Glenys here: http://www.pagaian.org.
.

Glenys introduced me to Korean, **Helen Hye-Sook Hwang, PhD**
Helen, who currently lives in California, founded **the Mago Academy - Magoism, The Way of We in S/He**. My artwork appears in several Mago publications
http://www.magoacademy.org.

New Zealander, **Jane Cunningham**, feels like a sister.
Find her artistic & mythic work here: https://www.numinousjane.com
We share kinship with Philadelphian D'Vorah Horn who began Mending Spirit:
http://www.D'Vorahhorn.com

Pennsylvanian, **Trebbe Johnson**, founded Radical Joy for Hard Times,
and got me started making beauty in wounded places.
https://www.radicaljoyforhardtimes.com

Arizonian, **Connie Solera** inspired me to paint both BIG and *DEEP*.
http://www.dirtyfootprints-studio.com

Oregonian, **Judy Todd**, began NatureConnect. Her devotion to serving life touches me. Find her programs here: https://www.natureconnectnw.com

Californian, **Cynthia Jurs**, brings an ancient tradition alive again,
blessing the earth with prayers of love and protection in a global mandala of buried Earth Treasure Vases. (ETV) http://earthtreasurevase.org/

Californian, **David Nicol,** supports the ETV program with monthly global full moon meditations with him and Cynthia. **Everyone is welcome to participate in these live broadcasts. Please join us**. David also creates his own programs:
http://gaiafield.net/events-home/ & https://subtleactivism.net/

Catherine Svehla, PhD, Californian, storyteller, podcaster and ceremonialist, lights my fire. Visit her here: www.mythinthemojave.com

Gail Warner, MA, MFT founded Pine Manor Retreat Center in California
www.pinemanor.com and has written a book of poetry which includes
a few of my Gaian images superimposed with her photography. Her potent voice is revelatory: Weaving Myself Awake – Voicing the Sacred Through Poetry.

Jill Chesrow from Illinois inspired me with her ability to manifest her dreams.
She guided 39 global artists in the creation of an oracle deck: **Awakening to your Divine Self** with a new deck forthcoming. http://www.fearless-sisters.com

Oregonian, **Dana Lynne Andersen**, lives part of each year in Italy where she is the Creative Director of the Academy of Art, Creativity and Consciousness.
www.awakeningartsacademy.com

Oregonian, **Stephanie Mines,** envisioned the Climate Change and Consciousness Conference scheduled for Findhorn, Scotland in 2019. May it awaken us all.
https://ccc19.org/

Evolution biologist and author, **Elisabet Sahtouris,** taught me about imaginal cells in 1989. Please read her recent book: Gaia's Dance: The Story of Earth & Us.
To learn more about Elisabet: http://www.sahtouris.com/

I am indebted to Margaret Bullitt-Jonas and Robert Jonas for introducing me to the term Expressive Prayer. http://revivingcreation.org

A big thank you to the **Friday writers' group** with whom I meet every other week.
Barbara, Carol, Donna, Lynne, Kathryn & Sandi.
Thank you for your inspiration, generosity and holding me accountable.
Specific gratitude wings to Carol for helping me take this plunge
and to Sandi for hearing imaginal cell as imaginal self.

Read Jeremy Lent's opus:
The Patterning Instinct - A Cultural History of Humanity's Search for Meaning.
www.liology.org

Most important, I am blessed by my four adult children, their spouses, and their children. It is for them that I write and paint to encourage us humans to grow up while we still can. Our planet's ability to support life, specifically human life, demands a revolution in how we live, what we value. With the depth and breadth of spirit, unprecedented scientific knowledge, and the technology now available, we can discover ways of being human never before known. Imagine living with a whole brain, an awakened *bodymind*, and a keen recognition that Earth is a living being with whom we dance. May we elders support the younger generations by bridging the richness of our past with the wonders of our future, opening portals to birth our imaginal selves and thus the eco-centric human.

Image Titles

Some originals are still available for purchase. All images are available as reproductions. Please inquire.

Cover— Detail Earth Rising
Title page - Gaia # 69— original cover for handcrafted limited edition <u>Ode to Gaia</u>
3. Gaia # 83: S/He Who Knows Where We Are
5. #88: S/He Who is Truly PaGaian
7. #81: First Family—They Who Carry our Ancestors Forward
9. #44: They Who Choose new Ways of Relating
11. #80: S/He Who Sees Cosmos in Chaos
13. Earth Rising
15. #47: S/He Who Brings the Sun
17. #32: Phoenix—S/He Who Rises Up Strong
19. #10: Perpetuity—S/He Who Orchestrates the Weather
21. #51: S/He Who Has Stars in her Eyes
23. #8: Constancy—S/He Who Tends the Forest
25. #72: Benediction—We Who Are All Bless-ed
27. #84: Black Madonna—S/He Who Glories in Interbeing
29. #64: S/He Who Breathes
31. #67: S/He Who Longs to Return Home
33. #2: Wild Salmon Woman—S/He Who Releases the Fish to the Sea
35. #5: S/He Who Bears the Burdens of Spring
37. #85: S/He Who Is Connected
39. #50: S/He Who Steps into Life
41. #46: S/He Who Hears the Whales Cry
43. #70: S/He Who Bestows Grace
45. #6: S/He Who Gives Voice to their Stories
47. #49: S/He Who Bears with Me
49. #7: S/He Who Watches Now
51. #78: S/He Who Tends the Bees and the Butterflies
53. #86: S/He Who Embraces Each New Day
55. #48: S/He Who Soars into New Possibilities
57. #89: S/He Who Remains Whole Despite Onslaught
58. #94: S/He Who Births the Imaginal Self
64. #90: S/He Who Is at Home in Her Neighborhood

We are here:
Awakening Storylines Press
Bainbridge Island, WA
deborahmltn@gmail.com

Made in the USA
Columbia, SC
29 November 2021

49646624R00038